ADHD in Girls:

Thriving with ADHD

Lucas Olle

Table of content

Chapter 1
Chapter 2
Chapter 3
Chapter 4

Chapter 1

ADHD in females — especially if it's the inattentive variety of ADHD previously termed ADD — might look like this:

daydreaming silently in class\sfeeling uncomfortable or sad\sexhibiting silliness or seeming ditziness\sacting bashful or inattentive\strouble sustaining friendships

plucking at cuticles or skin\sbeing a perfectionist

ADHD in Girls is Often Missed

Twenty-year-old Andrea Burns meets the criteria of ADHD in females completely. She wasn't formally diagnosed with attention deficit hyperactivity disorder (ADHD or ADD) until her freshman year at Indiana University, even though she displayed evident indicators of ADHD in middle school.

After Burns almost dropped out of school, an academic counselor had her take a LASSI (Learning and Studies Strategy Inventory) screening to examine learning practices and academic success. The findings showed what she and her family had long suspected: ADHD.

"In high school, I had a tutor to assist me with various classes, but once I came to college, I was supposed to complete it all by myself. I was studying all of the time, but performing terribly on examinations because I'd freeze up," recalls Burns. "And I'd attempt to listen in class, but I had a terrible time concentrating and focused on what the instructor was saying. I'd take loads of notes, but when I read them, I couldn't make sense of what I wrote," says the communications student, now approaching her junior year.

After a diagnosis of ADHD - Primarily Inattentive Type, Burns was administered ADHD medication. She experienced nearly immediate results: "I was finally able to concentrate during a lecture and take decent notes, which helped boost my scores. For the first time I felt in charge in the classroom."

Burns is glad to have found the root of her low school performance, and delighted she's able to fix it. But it's unjust that she, like so many other girls, spent a decade or more with an undiagnosed disease that may badly effect life in so many ways. Why are females being diagnosed so much later than boys, if at all? And what do teachers, doctors, and parents need to do to bring about a change?

Symptoms of ADHD in Girls

One of the primary reasons girls are so frequently missed is that they express hyperactivity differently than boys, according to Patricia Quinn, M.D., director of the National Center for Gender Issues and ADHD in Washington, D.C. "In a school situation, a guy would frequently blurt out answers or persistently stamp his foot, while a girl might display hyperactivity by chattering incessantly," she explains. A girl who speaks all the time is frequently perceived by the instructor as talkative, not hyper or troublesome — and therefore is less likely to be nominated for an assessment.

Another reason why ADHD is frequently ignored in females is that they're more likely than boys to suffer from inattentive ADHD. The symptoms of this sub-type (which include poor attention to detail, short attention span, forgetfulness, distractibility, and inability to complete assigned duties) tend to be less disruptive and visible than those of hyperactive ADHD. Put simply, a (hyperactive) lad who continuously knocks on his desk will be seen before the (inattentive) girl who twirls her hair while looking out the window. "I feel I was missed for so long because I didn't demonstrate hyperactivity the way my two brothers with ADHD have," says Burns.

Why ADHD in Girls Goes Undiagnosed

It comes as no surprise that a new national online Harris Interactive survey reinforces that, with relation to ADHD, females have gone mostly neglected. Dr. Quinn and Sharon Wigal, Ph.D., associate clinical professor of pediatrics at the University of California at Irvine, surveyed 3,234 people, including members of the general public (adults without ADHD whose children don't have the condition), parents of children with the condition, teachers, and children with ADHD, ages 12 to 17. Among those questioned, 85 percent of the instructors and more than half of the parents and the general public thought that females with ADHD are more likely to go undiagnosed. They claimed that females are more prone to "suffer silently" or display less symptoms. And four out of 10 instructors have greater difficulties in diagnosing ADHD symptoms in females than in boys.

Polled parents and teachers also reported that, among children with ADHD, males are more likely than girls to demonstrate behavioral difficulties, while girls are more frequently inattentive or coping with a mood illness. Drs. Quinn and Wigal said these variances lead some females with ADHD to slip through the gaps. "The inability to diagnose ADHD symptoms in females definitely leads in considerable undertreatment," they stated. "...it is not a small disorder for them, and they are similarly in need of competent care."

Girls with ADHD Face Serious Risks

Another discovery from the Harris poll: Females may experience greater negative impacts from having ADHD than their male counterparts. The poll found that females are more likely than boys to be ordered to repeat a grade owing to poor academic performance. When a male suffers, he's more likely to be checked for ADHD or LD (and subsequently diagnosed) than kept back. But a teacher who watches a disorderly female student — one who can't plan ahead, fulfill project deadlines, and so on — feels that she'll benefit from being held back a year. "A year later, the girl is no better off because she still hasn't worked out the basis of her problems," says Dr. Quinn.

The self-esteem of girls with ADHD also seems to be more impacted than that of males with ADHD (this may explain why the study indicated that girls were three times more likely to report using antidepressants prior to being diagnosed) (which may explain why the survey found that girls were three times more likely to report taking antidepressants prior to being diagnosed). It's hardly surprising, however, that the disease may take a toll on a female's mental health and overall well-being. According to Dr. Quinn, females with ADHD tend to have more mood disorders, anxiety, and self-esteem difficulties than non-ADHD girls. "They could receive an A on a paper, but since they had to work three times as hard to acquire it, they regard themselves as not being as brilliant as other people," she adds.

Another reason why females go undiscovered for so long has to do with how differently each gender approaches education. Dr. Quinn presents this example: "A male and female student with ADHD are given a long-term assignment. They each put off the assignment for weeks. Then, the night before the project is due, each recalls the deadline. Rather than try to get the job done, the boy chooses to watch back-to-back episodes of SpongeBob. Meanwhile, the girl panic out and strives to construct a flawless project overnight. (Perfectionism is another prevalent characteristic among ADHD females.) She requests that her mother assist her while she stays up until 1 a.m. to do her task. When she brings in the work the following day, the instructor has no indication that it was done at the last minute."

Girls appear obliged to get their academics done because our society pushes them to be more socially aware. They desire to please more than boys, and they're expected to perform well in school.

Because grades K through six aren't as challenging as higher grades, a girl with undiagnosed ADHD might do fine in elementary school — and then falter. "In middle and high school, the attentional demands are greater for a student, so she can't get by working at 50 percent efficiency," says Andrew Adesman, M.D., director of the division of behavioral and developmental disorders at Schneider's Children's Hospital in New Hyde Park, New York, and member of the national board of directors for CHADD. "And since the youngsters in junior high and high school more regularly change classrooms, instructors don't have the chance to get to know the kids and notice problems."

Some females may compensate by adopting tactics that disguise their ADHD. As indicated previously, it may be perfectionism. For instance, a girl could spend hours taking notes on each chapter she's being tested on in order to secure a decent mark. Or she can become obsessive-compulsive, checking and rechecking her bag to make sure she has everything.

ADHD gender inequalities also show up beyond the classroom. Research suggests that females with ADHD may be rejected more frequently by their classmates than boys. The fundamental reason is because, compared to boys', girls' friendships need higher complexity and more upkeep. "Two boys may meet on the playground and start digging a hole to China with their shovels, and they're immediate pals. Friendship among females is more challenging, especially at early ages. It takes picking up on social signs and bonding," explains Dr. Quinn.

With inclinations toward impulsivity, hyperactivity, and forgetfulness, it might be hard to keep your lips closed, not to continuously interrupt, or to remember your closest friend's birthday. And when everyone in the group is admiring Jessica's new earrings and the girl with ADHD blurts out something utterly irrelevant, the other girls stare at her and wonder where she's coming from. This kind of social awkwardness makes it difficult for a girl to feel good about herself and sustain relationships.

Chapter 2

Helping Girls with ADHD

If parents think that their daughter has ADHD (or a learning issue), Drs. Quinn and Wigal encourage them not to wait, even if teachers haven't voiced concern. As indicated previously, instructors frequently look for hyperactivity, disorganization, or forgetfulness as the indicators of ADHD before requesting an examination. But the way ADHD commonly presents itself in females — excessive talking, low self-esteem, fretting, perfectionism, risk-taking, and nosiness

At the age of 21, I gladly accomplished my ambition of reporting for a prominent daily newspaper. I was receiving loads of front-page articles, until I began making silly blunders. Most were small — misspelled names and the like — but then came a doozy: I unintentionally misquoted a prosecutor, making it appear like he'd charged someone with a murder when he hadn't.

Fearful, with good cause, that I was harming my career, I sought expert treatment. Given the period — the early 1980s — it meant that I laid on a psychiatrist's couch for many months and whined about my upbringing. I'd never even heard of ADHD in females. Meanwhile, I adopted the more realistic approach of teaching myself to read every word I wrote for publication at least three times before I filed it.

One or both of these techniques succeeded, and my career progressed on, unscathed by mishaps. But in 2007, I went to my former doctor, wanting treatment once more. I'd switched from international reporting to raising two kids in the suburbs, writing novels and magazine pieces in whatever time I had. But I was having far too many disagreements with my husband and kids, and I could never locate my keys — or sunglasses, or pencils, or dozens of other things.

How the world had changed! This time, instead of the sofa and the complaints, there was simply one appointment. After spending many hours in the doctor's office, he decided that there was a strong likelihood

I had ADHD. He recommended a stimulant to cure it.

Looking at my life through my new ADHD lens cleared solved decades of mystery regarding my behaviour. At finally I realized why my parents used to nickname me Chatty Kathy, and why I've lost so much excellent jewelry over the years, not to mention other basics. It also granted me membership into a shockingly wide group of once puzzled, midlife women who've achieved comparable discoveries.

ADHD Diagnosis Rates in Women and Girls

Barely 35 years after "Attention Deficit Disorder" first appeared in the bible of psychiatry, the Diagnostic and Statistical

Manual of Mental Disorders (DSM), front-line clinical therapists claim that rising awareness of the illness has led to many more girls being diagnosed when they're young. Even yet, although girls and boys presently are diagnosed at a ratio of roughly 1 to 3 — up from about 1 to 8 in the 1990s — the rate for diagnoses of adult women and men is about 1 to 1.

"It's just a matter of time until we learn this is an equal-opportunity condition, but a less glaringly visible one for girls," says psychologist and author Kathleen Nadeau, Ph.D., a pioneering authority on women with ADHD.

That's not a unique perspective, nor is it unanimous. Experts include psychologist

Stephen Hinshaw, Ph.D., leader of a large longitudinal study of girls with ADHD, and psychologist and author Russell A. Barkley, Ph.D., feel the 1 to 3 ratio of girls to boys diagnosed with the disorder is true. "Boys appear to be more sensitive to psychopathology," Hinshaw adds, noting rates of childhood autism that are also considerably higher for boys — on the order of 5 to 1.

Hinshaw, author of The Triple Bind: Saving Our Teenage Girls from Today's Pressures, speculates that greater incidence of ADHD in adult women could be explained by women having a form of the illness that lasts longer than it does in boys.

It's well known by now, he explains, that boys with ADHD are more likely than girls to demonstrate hyperactivity and impulsivity. More females than boys are diagnosed with the "inattentive," day-dreamy variant of the illness. Yet multiple longitudinal studies demonstrate that signs of activity wane throughout adolescence, although underlying issues with attention and organizing abilities frequently linger until adulthood.

Still, other variables could possibly explain why the male-female ratios alter in maturity, Hinshaw notes. Perhaps women are more honest than males about attention difficulties in maturity. Moreover, he feels that Nadeau and other specialists may be accurate in stating that many young females with ADHD are beneath the radar, to be recognized only as adults.

Indeed, hyperactivity, and frequently violence, goes along with many instances of ADHD. It generally gets more guys with ADHD discovered, and addressed, whereas ladies turn their rage inside. The consequence for women is years of poor self-confidence and psychological trauma.

How Undiagnosed ADHD Puts Girls at Risk

"Girls with ADHD are in severe jeopardy in a number of ways," adds Hinshaw. He and his colleagues reviewed data from 10-year, follow-up interviews of 140 girls who were aged 7 to 12 when originally polled. His findings, together with other studies gathered over five years, demonstrate that females with ADHD are at dramatically elevated risk for issues ranging from poor academic success to drug and alcohol misuse, and even suicide attempts. Females, in general, experience larger rates of anxiety and mood problems than men, and it seems that the incidence is much more evident when ADHD is a component.

A research published in the Archives of General Psychiatry indicated that females with ADHD were at substantially greater risk than ordinary girls, or than boys with the disease, for clinical mood disorders and suicide attempts. Another investigation, published in the American Journal of Psychiatry, indicated that females with ADHD were more prone than others to engage in antisocial conduct, and to suffer from drug use disorders or anxiety.

What's evident from his follow-up, Hinshaw adds, is that females with ADHD share with boys the substantial risks of school failure, rejection by peers, and drug addiction. Unlike males, girls also have a particularly high risk for developing mental disorders, self-injuring behavior, and eating disorders. "In other words, females with ADHD tend to demonstrate a larger variety of problematic outcomes than do boys," he adds.

Hinshaw argues females are hurt by earlier, and more successful, socializing. They are schooled from an early age not to cause problems, and to mask faults and miscues. They direct their fury on themselves, rather than others. When I was an adolescent, my parents may have feared that I had a mood illness, but they never considered that I may have an attention deficit. And so it goes in many homes today. Girls with inattentive ADHD will usually be diagnosed later than boys, and for something altogether different.

Meanwhile, females with the hyperactive variant of ADHD are stigmatized more than boys with the same diagnosis. Kids on the playground see impulsivity and distraction as masculine. Boys are more likely to receive a pass from other students and instructors, particularly if their symptoms aren't severe. Girls get shunned.

For many young women, the anxiety, stress, and low self-esteem that comes with ADHD feels intolerable by early adulthood. The structure of school is gone, a good for males but a loss for girls, who fare better with rules and rituals, according to Hinshaw.

When women with ADHD marry and have kids, many of them encounter what psychiatrist and author Sari Solden calls "a dreadful wall of shame." Society demands incredible feats of memory and organization from parents, from keeping track of essential details like schools and physicians to coordinating meals and different schedules. And without therapy, or a "wife" of their own, many women can't cut it.

Chapter 3

Is ADHD in Girls and Women Hereditary?

ADHD is highly genetic, and many women seek therapy as adults because a light bulb goes out when they have a kid who is diagnosed. This was the situation with Joy Carr. Watching her adolescent son fill out his diagnostic questionnaire brought a rush of memories — of her own dirty lockers, misplaced textbooks, and instructors who dubbed her intelligent but lazy. Following an usual trend for young people with ADHD, Carr, who lives near Buffalo, New York, dropped out of college as a junior, got married at 22, and had her first kid one year later.

For many years, her household tasks overwhelmed her. She'd start off on a duty, from a list her husband provided, then get diverted, ending up with duties half-done. "I'd toss a load of clothes in and forget about it for days," recalls Carr. "By then, it would smell musty, so I'd wash it again. And then I'd forget about it again."

In 2007, however, Carr's life took a turn for the better once she acquired her ADHD diagnosis and began taking ADHD medication. "The screaming, rushing thoughts in my brain quieted down," she adds. That following year, she went back to college to earn her undergraduate degree. After dealing with her kid, she apologized to her mother for the anguish she brought her as a child.

Women recount heartbreaking experiences of turning up for diagnostics. Kathleen Nadeau, who diagnosed herself in her 30s, had been an undergraduate at four different universities. Sari Solden, who was 42 when she learned out she had ADHD, says her journals witness to decades of wondering what was wrong. Was she immature? Did she have a brain tumor? Narcolepsy? Trying stimulants after years without them was like "greasing my brain," Solden says. "I recall going to a dinner that night. I was asked a question, and I really recounted a story."

ADHD in Women: Different Gender, Different Treatment

ADHD not only exhibits distinct symptoms in males and girls, but also typically demands a different treatment plan, adds Nadeau. Both genders benefit from stimulant drugs, she adds, although girls may require therapy for anxiety. They typically cannot take stimulants without supplementary medicinal help.

Hinshaw says he's not certain that females need additional medicines to withstand stimulants, compared to boys. He observes that, to the degree that girls are prone to acquire mood disorders and anxiety, evidence-based cognitive behavioral therapy may be useful. Nadeau also proposes group therapy, as a gender-specific method, to enable girls and women to utilize their language talents to offer one another support, build coping mechanisms, and not feel alienated.

Nadeau and her colleague, doctor Patricia Quinn, M.D., have been attempting to convince their colleagues to use a diagnostic instrument with symptoms that would assist more females comprehend that they potentially have ADHD. Nadeau says she's not hopeful that such reform will arrive in time for the next edition of the DSM.

Hinshaw's study, as well as other research that follows girls into adulthood, offers hope for more interventions over time, but, for now, parents and teachers have to work to help girls who are struggling with distraction — spotting them at home and in classrooms, and supporting them in getting diagnoses, even if they may not precisely fit the symptom profile.

Women with ADHD should share the message. While a little hardship makes you stronger, think what women with ADHD might do if we could transfer the energy we use to beat ourselves up to going out and improving the world.

ADHD Symptoms Checklist for Females\sPsychologist Kathleen Nadeau has designed a symptoms checklist for girls suspected of having ADHD. It should be filled out by females themselves, not parents and instructors, since girls feel ADHD more inwardly than boys, who attract attention through disorderly conduct.

Many of Nadeau's questions relate to boys, as they deal to issues with productivity, general distractibility, impulsivity, hyperactivity, and sleep disorders. The portions that follow, however, are primarily directed at girls:

Anxiety and mood problems

I frequently feel like I want to weep.

I have a lot of stomachaches or headaches.

I worry a lot.

I feel depressed, and sometimes I don't even know why.

School anxiety

I hate getting called on by the instructor because, typically, I haven't been listening closely.

I feel ashamed in class when I don't know what the instructor ordered us to do.

Even when I have something to say, I don't raise my hand and volunteer in class.

Social-skill deficiencies

Sometimes, other females don't like me, but I don't know why.

I had conflicts with my buddies.

When I want to join a group of females, I don't know how to approach them, or what to say.

I frequently feel left out.

Emotional over-reactivity

I get my emotions wounded more than other females.

My sentiments alter a lot.

I get furious and angry more than other females.

Parents & Teachers: Does This Sound Like a Girl You Know?

Five warning symptoms that your kid or student may have ADHD – according to Kathleen Nadeau:

Does she routinely misplace personal stuff, her keys, or her backpack?

Is her room constantly dirty — even 15 minutes after you clean it up?

Does she regularly feel nervous about getting her assignments in on time?

Does she speak excessively?

Does she behave nicely at school, and come home and erupt at the end of the day? Can she be driven over the brink by petty provocation?

Your daughter's physician may be able to undertake an assessment (if your daughter is a teenager, find out beforehand whether the doctor is familiar dealing with adolescents), but it's preferable to consult with an ADHD expert. Make sure the assessing doctor obtains a full medical history (including family history, owing to the significant heredity of ADHD) (including family history, due to the high heritability of ADHD). The doctor should also communicate with your child's school to acquire additional information about her behaviour. "And because teenagers are a tremendous source of knowledge regarding their personal experience, urge a teen to discuss directly with her doctor," suggests Dr. Wigal.

Ultimately, for a girl suffering with ADHD, a formal diagnosis might be wonderful news. "Everyone presumes that a diagnosis of ADHD is a stigma," says Dr. Quinn. "In fact, 56 percent of the girls in our poll reported that they felt better after finally having a term for what they felt. Only 15 percent indicated they felt worse. For most, it was a relief to find out they weren't lazy, insane, or stupid."

More good news: Parents of girls diagnosed with ADHD are most likely to seek treatment than parents of boys diagnosed with ADHD, since only the more severe instances are identified. "Girls may be at a minor advantage over males in one sense," wrote Quinn and Wigal in the Harris survey study. "Once kids are suspected of having ADHD, their parents tend to be more ready to seek medical advice." And it bodes good for girls.

20 Signs and Symptoms of ADHD in Females\sADHD symptoms in girls might

seem extremely different than they do in boys

Attention deficit hyperactivity disorder (ADHD) has long been considered of as a problem affecting men. But more girls are getting diagnosed as our knowledge of it grows. This is due, in part, to discovering that ADHD in females might seem different than it does in boys.

For instance, females are more prone to develop inattentive ADHD, in which daydreaming and shyness are typical. Conversely, it is more usual for males to have hyperactive-impulsive ADHD or combination type ADHD. 1

If left untreated, ADHD in females may result in disadvantages such as a lack of accommodation in the classroom, poor self-esteem, and self-blame. It may even impair mental health far into adulthood. Being aware of the varied signs of ADHD in girls will help you realize when it might be time to consult a doctor for an examination.

The State of Mental Health in Teen Girls

ADHD Symptoms in Girls

ADHD symptoms in females are typically thought of as personality qualities rather than ADHD, which is why they are often neglected or explained away. But what exactly does ADHD look like in females vs. boys? Here are a few signs to consider:

Appears withdrawn

Cries readily

Daydreaming and in a world of her own
\sDifficulty sustaining attention; easily
distracted

Disorganized and untidy (in both
appearance and physical space) (in both
appearance and physical space)

Doesn't seem to be attempting

Doesn't appear motivated

Forgetful

Highly sensitive to sounds, textures, and
emotions

Hyper-talkative (always has much to say, but is not excellent at listening) (always has lots to say, but is not good at listening)

Hyperreactivity (exaggerated emotional responses) (exaggerated emotional responses)

Looks to be making "careless" errors

Might frequently slam her doors shut

Often late (poor time management) (poor time management)

Problems completing assignments

Seems shy

Seems to become quickly offended

Shifting concentration from one task to another\sTakes time to comprehend information and directives; appears like she doesn't hear you\sVerbally impulsive; blurts out and interrupts others

Girls with ADHD won't necessarily have all these indications.

2 At the same time, having one or two symptoms does not guarantee that ADHD is definite.

If your daughter, grandchild, or another young girl in your life shows a couple of these signs on a constant basis, a chat with an experienced expert may be useful.

ADHD symptoms might present differently in each kid. You may have one kid who has been diagnosed with ADHD, but never thought that the other may also have it since their challenges appear so different.

Diagnosing ADHD in Girls

It is much simpler to imagine that a kid who is physically active and disobedient would benefit from an ADHD examination more so than a youngster who looks distant or preoccupied. But, among females, ADHD indications and symptoms seem to share a few underlying similarities.

Compensates for Inattention

For many females with ADHD, paying attention to the work at hand is their toughest struggle. They might become distracted by external events or drift off into a world of their own. For example, a bird outside a classroom window may divert attention away from something more significant in their surroundings, like a teacher stating the date of an approaching test.

To compensate, a girl with ADHD may hyperfocus on something she enjoys or is skilled at. She will put out so much effort and focus into that one item that parents or instructors may disregard the likelihood of ADHD.

Sometimes, her hyperfocus is a coping tactic to keep oneself amused when something is dull. Other times, she may not feel she has any control over it.

Always in Motion

If a girl is hyperactive, she could be labeled as a "tomboy" since she appreciates physical activity and doesn't appear to like the same things as other females her age. ADHD in girls could also show itself in less noticeable ways that nonetheless include continuously being in motion, such as by sketching continually or always moving about in her chair.

Lack of Impulse Control

A girl with ADHD may exhibit impulsivity and be hyper-talkative. She may be verbally impetuous, interrupt people, speak excessively, or shift subjects often during talks. She could even blurt forth remarks without thinking about their effect on others.

Girls with ADHD can also be overly sensitive. Some are described as overemotional and easily excitable.

Getting Treatment for Girls With ADHD

A mental health expert may perform the testing required to discover if the girl in your life may have ADHD and get treatment started. Treatment for ADHD in females might involve behavior control approaches, organizational measures, medication, counseling, and support.

Simply understanding she has ADHD may relieve a young girl of a heavy load of guilt and shame. It may also release her from the negative labels of being "spacey," "unmotivated," "stupid," or "lazy."

A girl with ADHD is none of those things. She just has ADHD. And solutions may be put in place to make her life a bit simpler and her future brighter. The first step to make this happen is identifying the distinct ADHD symptoms in females, and now you know what to look for

Chapter 4

Understanding ADHD in girls

Parents and other caregivers could begin to suspect ADHD in boys who:\scan't sit still in school\sdisrupt learning by repeatedly shouting out of turn\sspend hours playing video games but become angry after a few minutes of homework

They may not notice or search for comparable behaviors in females, but girls generally don't display such indicators, too.

Instead, maybe your daughter:

reads far ahead in the novel assigned for class but consistently fails to do the homework questions\sspends hours working on math homework but often forgets to turn it in\ssits quietly in class, doodling in her notebook instead of paying attention and taking notes\shas trouble making and keeping friends\sconstantly seems lost in her own thoughts\sis often called a "chatterbox" by teachers and other adults

In summary, ladies with ADHD could look preoccupied, dreamy, or forgetful instead being openly disruptive. As a consequence, caregivers frequently don't recognize the link, particularly in the absence of hyperactive or disruptive behavior.

Girls are also more likely to compensate for symptoms with coping strategies like:\sspending extra time to get schoolwork and chores just right\savoiding people, tasks, or events they find challenging\screating conflict to deflect attention from any problems they're having\schecking work or tasks repeatedly to make sure they're complete and correct

These coping tactics could give some short-term advantages, but they don't always work. Sometimes, they may even cause further issues – like making ADHD symptoms more harder to identify.

Risk factors for ADHD

While specialists haven't discovered one precise cause of ADHD, they do know some variables that contribute to the illness.

Factors that can raise your child's chances of getting ADHD include:\sfamily history, or having a parent or sibling with the condition\sprenatal or childhood exposure to lead and certain pesticides

prenatal exposure to alcohol or tobacco\strauma or harm to the brain

early birth or having a lower birth weight

Possible complications

ADHD symptoms frequently don't improve without treatment, and untreated ADHD might worsen over time. Even lesser symptoms may create lots of anxiety and impact everyday life at school or home, and with friendships and relationships.

Plus, females who never acquire a diagnosis may wind up blaming themselves for the challenges they endure. Instead of embracing these sensations as evidence of a mental health disorder that needs professional help, individuals might:\sfeel upset with their lack of success. think they need to work harder\sfrequently feel overwhelmed and drained by their efforts\swonder why they "can't do anything right". have trouble reaching objectives and lose their enthusiasm to keep trying. Over time, this internalization may impact self-esteem and self-worth. It may also lead to self-punishment and an overall feeling of despair.

Other possible issues include:

constant difficulty in relationships with parents, teachers, and friends

rejection or abuse from classmates and peers

Trusted Source

social isolation, or few intimate friendships greater likelihood of eating disorders chronic sleep troubles

problems excelling at school or work\sincreased probability of other mental health concerns, including drug use disorders and depression. It's also important bearing in mind that therapy for anxiety, sadness, and other mental health symptoms could have less impact when ADHD symptoms go ignored.

Coexisting conditions

ADHD doesn't create other psychological or developmental difficulties. However, children with ADHD are more likely than others to also have illnesses such as:

Oppositional defiant disorder (ODD), often characterized as a pattern of unpleasant, rebellious and aggressive conduct toward authority figures Conduct disorder, characterised by antisocial conduct such as stealing, fighting, damaging property, and injuring people or animals. Disruptive mood dysregulation disorder, characterized by impatience and issues with irritation

Learning impairments, including difficulty with reading, writing, comprehending and communicating Substance use disorders, including drugs, alcohol and smoking Anxiety disorders, which may induce excessive concern and uneasiness, and include obsessive compulsive disorder (OCD) (OCD)

Mood disorders, include depression and bipolar disorder, which involves depression as well as manic behavior Autism spectrum disease, a condition connected to brain development that alters how a person sees and socializes with others. Tic disorder or Tourette syndrome, diseases that entail repeated motions or unpleasant sounds (tics) that can't be readily controlled